William Makepeace Thackeray, Howard Pyle

The Chronicle of the Drum

William Makepeace Thackeray, Howard Pyle

The Chronicle of the Drum

ISBN/EAN: 9783743349957

Manufactured in Europe, USA, Canada, Australia, Japa

Cover: Foto ©ninafisch / pixelio.de

Manufactured and distributed by brebook publishing software (www.brebook.com)

William Makepeace Thackeray, Howard Pyle

The Chronicle of the Drum

The Chronicle of the Drum

By William Makepeace Thackeray

New-York
Charles Scribner's Sons
1882

⁎ *This Ballad was written in Paris, in 1841, at the time of the Second Funeral of Napoleon.*

ILLUSTRATIONS

	Artist.	Engraver.	Page.
"Ho, drummer! quick, silence yon Capet," Says Santerre, "with a beat of your drum." Lustily then did I tap it, And the son of St. Louis was dumb	Pyle	French	Frontispiece
Portrait of Thackeray	Laurence	Closson	Title
Ornamental title. Part I	Geo. Gibson	T. Hellawell	1
On the sunshiny bench of a tavern He sits and he prates of old wars	Frost	J. Hellawell	2

vii

	Artist	Engraver	Page

My ancestors drummed for King Harry,
    The Huguenot Lad of Navarre.................Fredericks.....Karst......... 4

The news it was brought to King Louis;
    Corblen! How his Majesty swore!..............Lungren.......Closson....... 6

• • • • Louis the Great,—
    Old, lonely, and half broken-hearted...........Fredericks.....Karst......... 8

At Rossbach, in spite of dad's drumming,
    'Tis said we were beaten by Fritz..............Taber.........Heinemann... 11

• • • The good town of Quebec ....Schell.........Geyer......... 12

Dear mammy she looks in their faces,
    And asks if her husband is come?
He is lying all cold on the glacis,
    And will never more beat on the drum..........Frost..........E. Clement.... 14

• • The lovely court-ladies in powder,
    And lappets, and long satin-tails..............Lungren.......Closson....... 17

viii

	Artist.	Engraver.	Page.
At her Majesty's opera-box	Lungren	J. P. Davis	19

And so *smiling* she looked and *so tender*,
That our officers, privates and drummers,
  All swore they would die to defend her..........Fredericks.....Karst.......... 20

And, like a majestical monarch,
  Kept filing his locks and his keys..............Fredericks.....Winham...... 23

We stormed and we broke the great gate in ....Share.........Evans........ 25

At midnight I beat the tattoo,
And woke up the pikemen of Paris
  To follow the bold Barbaroux...................Share.........French....... 27

* * The fair gardens where towered
  The walls of his heritage splendid..............J. S. Davis....Smart   28

I love to go sit in the sun there,
  The flowers and fountains to see................J. S. Davis...Annin........ 30

Awful, and proud, and erect,
  Here sat our republican goddess........ ......Pyle..........French....... 33

	Artist.	Engraver.	Page.
Young virgins with fair golden tresses, Old silver-hair'd prelates and priests	Fredericks	Karst	34
Ornamental title. Part II	Geo. Gibson	Andrew	37
She looked from the bars of her prison, And shriek'd as she saw it, and fell	Pyle	E. Clement	38
As she felt the foul fingers that touch'd her, She shrank, but she deigned not to speak	Birch	Wolf	41
* * * The Austrian flags Flaunt proud in the fields of Savoy	Woodward	J. Hellawell	43
The drummer now bared his old breast, And show'd us a plenty of scars	Frost	Karst	45
A Brunswicker made it at Jena, Beside the fair river of Saal	Taylor	Heinemann	47
Had winter not driven them back	Woodward	Andrew	49

x

	Artist.	Engraver.	Page.
* * He passed through the lines of his guard, And our drums beat the notes of salute	Taber	Held	53
The red-coats were crowning the height	Share	Heinemann	55
* * * * At sunset His banners were floating there still	Woodward	Andrew	57
I'll give you a curse on all traitors	Frost	Held	58
The grave historian at his desk	Taber	Heard	64

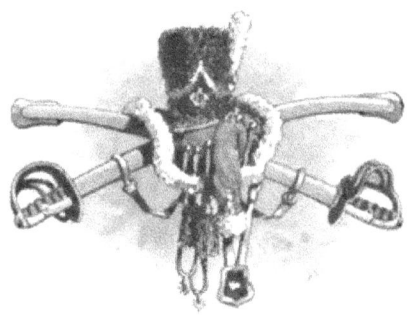

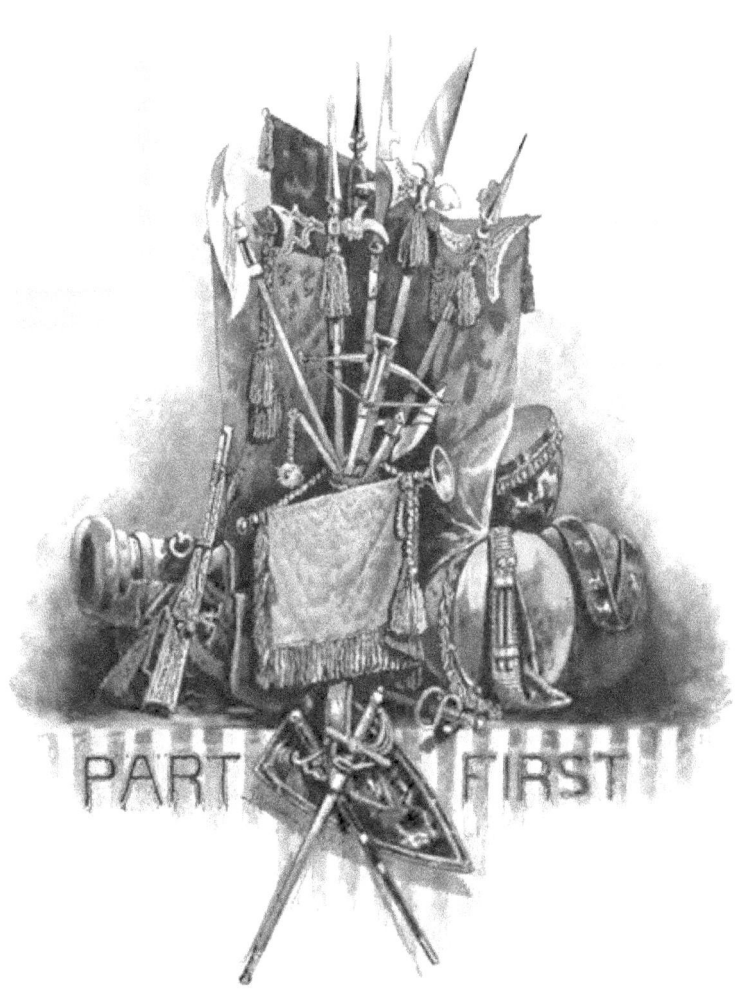

THE CHRONICLE OF THE DRUM.

At Paris, hard by the Maine barriers,
    Whoever will choose to repair,
Midst a dozen of wooden-legged warriors
    May haply fall in with old Pierre.
On the sunshiny bench of a tavern
    He sits and he prates of old wars,
And moistens his pipe of tobacco
    With a drink that is named after Mars.

The beer makes his tongue run the quicker,
    And as long as his tap never fails,
Thus over his favourite liquor
    Old Peter will tell his old tales.
Says he, "In my life's ninety summers
    Strange changes and chances I've seen,—
So here's to all gentlemen drummers
    That ever have thumped on a skin.

"Brought up in the art military
  For four generations we are;
My ancestors drumm'd for King Harry,
  The Huguenot lad of Navarre.
And as each man in life has his station
  According as Fortune may fix,
While Condé was waving the bâton,
  My grandsire was trolling the sticks.

"Ah! those were the days for commanders!
  What glories my grandfather won,
Ere bigots, and lackeys, and panders
  The fortunes of France had undone!
In Germany, Flanders, and Holland,—
  What foeman resisted us then?
No; my grandsire was ever victorious,
  My grandsire and Monsieur Turenne.

"He died: and our noble battalions
The jade fickle Fortune forsook;

And at Blenheim, in spite of our valiance,
  The victory lay with Malbrook.
The news it was brought to King Louis;
  Corbleu! how his Majesty swore
When he heard they had taken my grandsire:
  And twelve thousand gentlemen more.

"At Namur, Ramillies, and Malplaquet
  Were we posted, on plain or in trench:
Malbrook only need to attack it
  And away from him scamper'd we French.
Cheer up! 'tis no use to be glum, boys,—
  'Tis written, since fighting begun,
That sometimes we fight and we conquer,
  And sometimes we fight and we run.

"To fight and to run was our fate:
   Our fortune and fame had departed.
And so perish'd Louis the Great,—
   Old, lonely, and half broken-hearted.
His coffin they pelted with mud,
   His body they tried to lay hands on;
And so having buried King Louis
   They loyally served his great-grandson.

"God save the beloved King Louis!
   (For so he was nicknamed by some),
And now came my father to do his
   King's orders and beat on the drum.
My grandsire was dead, but his bones
   Must have shaken, I'm certain, for joy,
To hear daddy drumming the English
   From the meadows of famed Fontenoy.

"So well did he drum in that battle
   That the enemy show'd us their backs;
Corbleu! it was pleasant to rattle
   The sticks and to follow old Saxe!
We next had Soubise as a leader,
   And as luck hath its changes and fits,

At Rossbach, in spite of dad's drumming,
'Tis said we were beaten by Fritz.

"And now daddy cross'd the Atlantic,
　To drum for Montcalm and his men;
Morbleu! but it makes a man frantic
　To think we were beaten again!
My daddy he cross'd the wide ocean,
　My mother brought me on her neck,
And we came in the year fifty-seven
　To guard the good town of Quebec.

"In the year fifty-nine came the Britons,—
　Full well I remember the day,—
They knocked at our gates for admittance,
　Their vessels were moor'd in our bay.
Says our general, 'Drive me yon red-coats
　Away to the sea whence they come!'
So we march'd against Wolfe and his bull-dogs,
　We marched at the sound of the drum.

"I think I can see my poor mammy
  With me in her hand as she waits,
And our regiment, slowly retreating,
  Pours back through the citadel gates.
Dear mammy she looks in their faces,
  And asks if her husband is come?
He is lying all cold on the glacis,
  And will never more beat on the drum.

"Come, drink, 'tis no use to be glum, boys!
  He died like a soldier in glory;
Here's a glass to the health of all drum-boys,
  And now I'll commence my own story.
Once more did we cross the salt ocean,
  We came in the year eighty-one;
And the wrongs of my father the drummer
  Were avenged by the drummer his son.

"In Chesapeake Bay we were landed,
  In vain strove the British to pass:
Rochambeau our armies commanded,
  Our ships they were led by De Grasse.
Morbleu! how I rattled the drumsticks
  The day we march'd into Yorktown;
Ten thousand of beef-eating British
  Their weapons we caused to lay down.

"Then homewards returning victorious,
  In peace to our country we came,
And were thanked for our glorious actions
  By Louis, Sixteenth of the name.
What drummer on earth could be prouder
  Than I, while I drumm'd at Versailles

To the lovely court ladies in powder,
And lappets, and long satin-tails?

"The princes that day passed before us,
   Our countrymen's glory and hope;
Monsieur, who was learned in Horace,
   D'Artois, who could dance the tight-rope.
One night we kept guard for the Queen
   At her Majesty's opera-box,
While the King, that majestical monarch,
   Sat filing at home at his locks.

"Yes, I drumm'd for the fair Antoinette,
And so smiling she look'd and so tender,

That our officers, privates, and drummers,
  All vow'd they would die to defend her.
But she cared not for us honest fellows,
  Who fought and who bled in her wars,
She sneer'd at our gallant Rochambeau,
  And turned Lafayette out of doors.

"Ventrebleu! then I swore a great oath,
  No more to such tyrants to kneel;
And so, just to keep up my drumming,
  One day I drumm'd down the Bastile.
Ho, landlord! a stoup of fresh wine.
  Come, comrades, a bumper we'll try,
And drink to the year eighty-nine
  And the glorious fourth of July!

"Then bravely our cannon it thunder'd
  As onwards our patriots bore.
Our enemies were but a hundred,
  And we twenty thousand or more.
They carried the news to King Louis,
  He heard it as calm as you please,
And, like a majestical monarch,
  Kept filing his locks and his keys.

" We show'd our republican courage,
   We storm'd and we broke the great gate in,

And we murder'd the insolent governor
  For daring to keep us a-waiting.
Lambesc and his squadrons stood by:
  They never stirr'd finger or thumb.
The saucy aristocrats trembled
  As they heard the republican drum.

"Hurrah! what a storm was a-brewing!
  The day of our vengeance was come!
Through scenes of what carnage and ruin
  Did I beat on the patriot drum!
Let's drink to the famed tenth of August;
  At midnight I beat the tattoo,
And woke up the pikemen of Paris
  To follow the bold Barbaroux.

"With pikes, and with shouts, and with torches,
March'd onward our dusty battalions,

And we girt the tall castle of Louis,
   A million of tatterdemalions!
We storm'd the fair gardens where tower'd
   The walls of his heritage splendid.
Ah, shame on him, craven and coward,
   That had not the heart to defend it!

"With the crown of his sires on his head,
  His nobles and knights by his side,
At the foot of his ancestors' palace
  'Twere easy, methinks, to have died.
But no: when we burst through his barriers,
  'Mid heaps of the dying and dead,
In vain through the chambers we sought him—
  He had turn'd like a craven and fled.

*   *   *   *   *   *

"You all know the Place de la Concorde?
  'Tis hard by the Tuileries wall.
'Mid terraces, fountains, and statues,
  There rises an obelisk tall.
There rises an obelisk tall,
  All garnished and gilded the base is;
'Tis surely the gayest of all
  Our beautiful city's gay places.

"Around it are gardens and flowers,
    And the Cities of France on their thrones,
Each crown'd with his circlet of flowers
    Sits watching this biggest of stones!
I love to go sit in the sun there,
    The flowers and fountains to see,
And to think of the deeds that were done there
    In the glorious year ninety-three.

"'Twas here stood the Altar of Freedom;
  And though neither marble nor gilding
Was used in those days to adorn
  Our simple republican building,
Corbleu! but the MÈRE GUILLOTINE
  Cared little for splendor or show,
So you gave her an axe and a beam,
  And a plank and a basket or so.

"Awful, and proud, and erect,
  Here sat our republican goddess.
Each morning her table we deck'd
  With dainty aristocrats' bodies.
The people each day flocked around
  As she sat at her meat and her wine:
'Twas always the use of our nation
  To witness the sovereign dine.

"Young virgins with fair golden tresses,
Old silver-hair'd prelates and priests,

Dukes, marquises, barons, princesses,
  Were splendidly served at her feasts.
Ventrebleu! but we pamper'd our ogress
  With the best that our nation could bring,
And dainty she grew in her progress,
  And called for the head of a King!

"She called for the blood of our King,
  And straight from his prison we drew him;
And to her with shouting we led him,
  And took him, and bound him, and slew him.
'The monarchs of Europe against me
  Have plotted a godless alliance:
I'll fling them the head of King Louis,'
  She said, 'as my gage of defiance.'

"I see him as now, for a moment,
   Away from his gaolers he broke;
And stood at the foot of the scaffold,
   And linger'd, and fain would have spoke.
'Ho, drummer! quick, silence yon Capet,'
   Says Santerre, 'with a beat of your drum.'
Lustily then did I tap it,
   And the son of Saint Louis was dumb."

"THE glorious days of September
  Saw many aristocrats fall;
'Twas then that our pikes drank the blood
  In the beautiful breast of Lamballe.
Pardi, 'twas a beautiful lady!
  I seldom have look'd on her like;
And I drumm'd for a gallant procession,
  That marched with her head on a pike.

"Let's show the pale head to the Queen,
  We said—she'll remember it well.
She looked from the bars of her prison,
  And shriek'd as she saw it, and fell.

We set up a shout at her screaming,
   We laugh'd at the fright she had shown
At the sight of the head of her minion—
   How she'd tremble to part with her own!

"We had taken the head of King Capet,
   We called for the blood of his wife;
Undaunted she came to the scaffold,
   And bared her fair neck to the knife.
As she felt the foul fingers that touch'd her,
   She shrank, but she deigned not to speak:

She look'd with a royal disdain,
And died with a blush on her cheek!

" 'Twas thus that our country was saved ;
    So told us the safety committee!
But psha! I've the heart of a soldier,
    All gentleness, mercy, and pity.
I loathed to assist at such deeds,
    And my drum beat its loudest of tunes
As we offered to justice offended
    The blood of the bloody tribunes.

" Away with such foul recollections!
    No more of the axe and the block ;
I saw the last fight of the sections,
    As they fell 'neath our guns at Saint Rock.

Young Bonaparte led us that day;
   When he sought the Italian frontier,
I follow'd my gallant young captain,
   I follow'd him many a long year.

"We came to an army in rags,
   Our general was but a boy
When we first saw the Austrian flags
   Flaunt proud in the fields of Savoy.

In the glorious year ninety-six,
   We march'd to the banks of the Po;
I carried my drum and my sticks,
   And we laid the proud Austrian low.

" In triumph we enter'd Milan,
   We seized on the Mantuan keys;
The troops of the Emperor ran,
   And the Pope he fell down on his knees."—
Pierre's comrades here call'd a fresh bottle,
   And clubbing together their wealth,
They drank to the Army of Italy,
   And General Bonaparte's health.

The drummer now bared his old breast,
And show'd us a plenty of scars,

Rude presents that Fortune had made him
   In fifty victorious wars.
"This came when I follow'd bold Kleber—
   'Twas shot by a Mameluke gun;
And this from an Austrian sabre,
   When the field of Marengo was won.

"My forehead has many deep furrows,
   But this is the deepest of all:
A Brunswicker made it at Jena,
   Beside the fair river of Saal.
This cross, 'twas the Emperor gave it;
   (God bless him!) it covers a blow;
I had it at Austerlitz fight,
   As I beat on my drum in the snow.

" 'Twas thus that we conquer'd and fought ;
   But wherefore continue the story?
There's never a baby in France
   But has heard of our chief and our glory,—
But has heard of our chief and our fame,
   His sorrows and triumphs can tell,
How bravely Napoleon conquer'd,
   How bravely and sadly he fell.

" It makes my old heart to beat higher,
   To think of the deeds that I saw ;
I follow'd bold Ney through the fire,
   And charged at the side of Murat."
And so did old Peter continue
   His story of twenty brave years;
His audience follow'd with comments—
   Rude comments of curses and tears.

He told how the Prussians in vain
  Had died in defence of their land;
His audience laugh'd at the story,
  And vow'd that their captain was grand!
He had fought the red English, he said,
  In many a battle of Spain;
They cursed the red English, and prayed
  To meet them and fight them again.

He told them how Russia was lost,
  Had winter not driven them back;

And his company cursed the quick frost,
   And doubly they cursed the Cossack.
He told how the stranger arrived;
   They wept at the tale of disgrace;
And they long'd but for one battle more,
   The stain of their shame to efface.

"Our country their hordes overrun,
   We fled to the fields of Champagne,
And fought them, though twenty to one,
   And beat them again and again!
Our warrior was conquer'd at last;
   They bade him his crown to resign;
To fate and his country he yielded
   The rights of himself and his line.

" He came, and among us he stood,
  Around him we press'd in a throng:
We could not regard him for weeping,
  Who had led us and loved us so long.
'I have led you for twenty long years,'
  Napoleon said ere he went;
'Wherever was honour I found you,
  And with you, my sons, am content!

"'Though Europe against me was arm'd,
  Your chiefs and my people are true;
I still might have struggled with fortune,
  And baffled all Europe with you.

"'But France would have suffer'd the while,
   'Tis best that I suffer alone;
I go to my place of exile,
   To write of the deeds we have done.

"'Be true to the king that they give you.
   We may not embrace ere we part;
But, General, reach me your hand,
   And press me, I pray, to your heart.'

"He call'd for our battle standard;
   One kiss to the eagle he gave.
'Dear eagle!' he said, 'may this kiss
   Long sound in the hearts of the brave!'

"'Twas thus that Napoleon left us;
   Our people were weeping and mute,

As he passed through the lines of his guard,
And our drums beat the notes of salute.

"I look'd when the drumming was o'er,
   I look'd, but our hero was gone;
We were destined to see him once more,
   When we fought on the Mount of St. John.
The Emperor rode through our files;
   'Twas June, and a fair Sunday morn.
The lines of our warriors for miles
   Stretch'd wide through the Waterloo corn.

"In thousands we stood on the plain,
   The red-coats were crowning the height:
'Go scatter yon English,' he said;
   'We'll sup, lads, at Brussels to-night.'

We answer'd his voice with a shout;
  Our eagles were bright in the sun;
Our drums and our cannon spoke out,
  And the thundering battle begun.

"One charge to another succeeds,
  Like waves that a hurricane bears;
All day do our galloping steeds
  Dash fierce on the enemy's squares.
At noon we began the fell onset:
  We charged up the Englishman's hill;
And madly we charged it at sunset—
  His banners were floating there still.

"— Go to! I will tell you no more;
You know how the battle was lost.

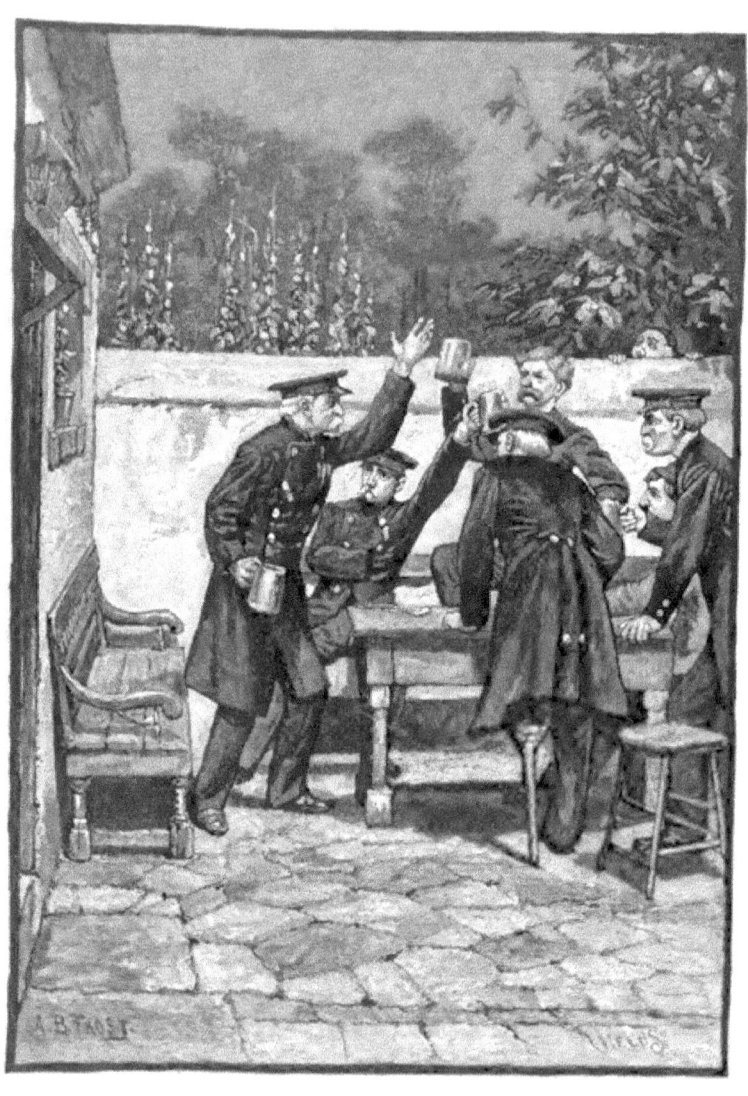

Ho! fetch me a beaker of wine,
  And, comrades, I'll give you a toast.
I'll give you a curse on all traitors,
  Who plotted our Emperor's ruin;
And a curse on those red-coated English,
  Whose bayonets helped our undoing.

" A curse on those British assassins,
  Who order'd the slaughter of Ney;
A curse on Sir Hudson, who tortured
  The life of our hero away.
A curse on all Russians—I hate them—
  On all Prussian and Austrian fry;
And oh! but I pray we may meet them,
  And fight them again ere I die."

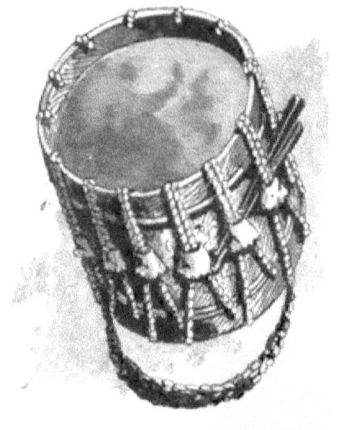

'Twas thus old Peter did conclude
    His chronicle with curses fit.
He spoke the tale in accents rude,
    In ruder verse I copied it.

Perhaps the tale a moral bears,
    (All tales in time to this must come),
The story of two hundred years
    Writ on the parchment of a drum.

What Peter told with drum and stick
    Is endless theme for poet's pen,—
Is found in endless quartos thick,
    Enormous books by learned men.

And ever since historian writ,
    And ever since a bard could sing,
Doth each exalt with all his wit
    The noble art of murdering.

We love to read the glorious page,
    How bold Achilles kill'd his foe;
And Turnus, fell'd by Trojans' rage,
    Went howling to the shades below.

How Godfrey led his red-cross knights,
    How mad Orlando slash'd and slew;
There's not a single bard that writes
    But doth the glorious theme renew.

And while, in fashion **picturesque,**
The poet rhymes of blood and blows,
The grave historian at his desk
Describes the same in classic prose.

Go read the works of Reverend Coxe,
You'll duly see recorded there
The history of the self-same knocks
Here roughly sung by Drummer Pierre.

Of battles fierce and warriors big,
He writes in phrases dull and slow,
And waves his cauliflower wig,
And shouts "St. George for Marlborow!"

*Take Doctor Southey from the shelf,
An LL. D.,—a peaceful man;
Good Lord, how doth he plume himself
Because we beat the Corsican!*

From first to last his page is filled
    With stirring tales how blows were struck.
He shows how we the Frenchmen kill'd,
    And praises God for our good luck.

Some hints, 'tis true, of politics
    The doctors give and statesman's art:
Pierre only bangs his drum and sticks,
    And understands the bloody part.

He cares not what the cause may be,
    He is not nice for wrong and right;
But show him where's the enemy,
    He only asks to drum and fight.

They bid him fight,—perhaps he wins;
  And when he tells the story o'er,
The honest savage brags and grins,
  And only longs to fight once more.

But luck may change, and valour fail,
  Our drummer, Peter, meet reverse,
And with a moral points his tale—
  The end of all such tales—a curse.

Last year, my love, it was my hap
  Behind a grenadier to be,
And, but he wore a hairy cap,
  No taller man, methinks, than me.

Prince Albert and the Queen, God wot,
  (Be blessings on the glorious pair!)
Before us passed. I saw them not—
  I only saw a cap of hair.

Your orthodox historian puts
  *In foremost rank the soldier **thus**,*
*The red-coat bully **in** his boots,*
  *That hides the march of men **from** us.*

*He puts him there in foremost **rank**,*
  ***You** wonder at his cap of hair·*
***You hear** his sabre's cursed clank,*
  ***His** spurs are jingling **everywhere**.*

Go to! I hate him and his trade:
  Who bade us so to cringe and bend,
And all God's peaceful people made
  To such as him subservient?

Tell me what find we to admire
  In epaulets and scarlet coats—
In men, because they load and fire,
  And know the art of cutting throats?

*   *   *   *   *   *

Ah, gentle, tender lady mine!
  The winter wind blows cold and shrill;
Come, fill me one more glass of wine,
  And give the silly fools their will.

And what care we for war and wrack,
  How kings and heroes rise and fall?
Look yonder, in his coffin black,
  There lies the greatest of them all!

To pluck him down, and keep him up,
  Died many million human souls.—
'Tis twelve o'clock and time to sup;
  Bid Mary heap the fire with coals.

He captured many thousand guns;
  He wrote "The Great" before his name;
And dying, only left his sons
  The recollection of his shame.

Though more than half the world was his,
  He died without a rood his own;
And borrow'd from his enemies
  Six foot of ground to lie upon.

He fought a thousand glorious wars,
  And more than half the world was his,
And somewhere now, in yonder stars,
  Can tell, mayhap, what greatness is.

www.ingramcontent.com/pod-product-compliance
Lightning Source LLC
Chambersburg PA
CBHW020338090426
42735CB00009B/1582